Designs for
Australian Birds
in Glass Windows

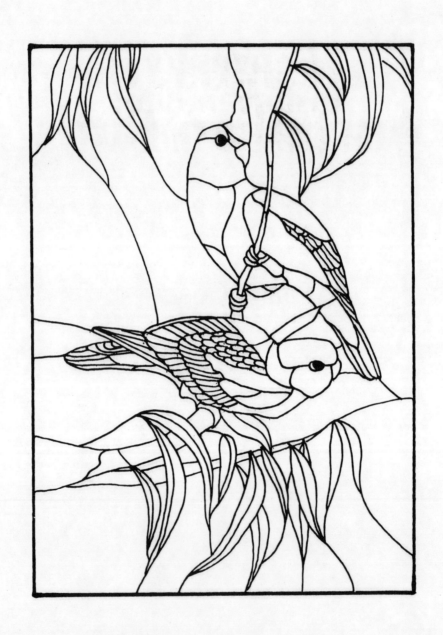

Designs for Australian Birds in Glass Windows

Diane Coady

Kangaroo Press

First published in 1993 by Kangaroo Press Pty Ltd
3 Whitehall Road (P.O. Box 75) Kenthurst 2156
Typeset by G.T. Setters Pty Limited
Printed in Hong Kong by Colorcraft Ltd

ISBN 0 86417 497 7

Contents

Foreword

The thirty-two designs in this book are suitable for working in both lead and copper foiling. Detailed instructions are given for working in lead. The designs can be made into suncatchers, using the copper foiling technique, following the instructions in my previous books from Kangaroo Press, *Australian Birds in Stained Glass* and *Australian Wildflowers in Stained Glass*.

There are many techniques for constructing lead panels and the instructions in this book are my method. No construction method is better or worse than any other, providing the resulting panel is strong, stable, weatherproof and neat.

I dedicate this book to my husband Neville and our daughter Sarah for their continuing support.

Debbie Lambley—once again, many thanks for all your help with your keyboard skills.

Glass-ary

Border lead   Lead that borders the panel. It fits into the rebate of the frame.

Calme   Strips of lead which hold glass within channels.

Cartoon   Full-sized design.

Cement   A compound used to seal and weatherproof leaded panels.

Cleaning compound   A mix of whiting and fine sawdust used to clean panels after puttying.

Flux   Product which helps solder to adhere to lead.

Jig   Removable timber frame that leaded panels are constructed within. Usually made of timber 10 cm (½'') by 30 cm (1½'') wide, and longer than the panel edges.

Leadlight   Glass pieces held together with lead.

Leadwork   Same as leadlight.

Master pattern   Full-sized pattern from which working cartoons are drawn.

Putty   Can be used in place of cement; made of different ingredients.

Solder   Solid core only is used: 60/40 solder containing 60% tin, 40% lead is best for leadlighting. Also available in 50/50 and 40/60. In America 63/37 is also available.

Stained glass   Glass that has been painted with stain or enamels and fired in a kiln. Commonly but wrongly used in reference to all methods of creating glass panels.

Making a full-sized pattern

1. After drawing up the correct panel size, enlarge the chosen design to the required size, either by the grid method illustrated in Fig. 1 or by using an enlarging photocopy machine. Remember copying can distort the design slightly.

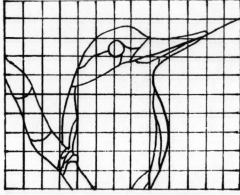

Fig. 1 *Using a graph to enlarge a pattern*

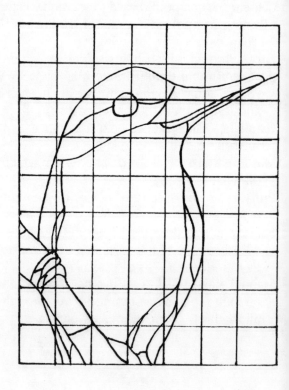

2. Some stained glass shops have computers which can enlarge and print out the design for you.
3. Transfer the enlarged design onto the drawn panel, into the glass viewing area. Take the design lines to the glass cutting edge. Use a black Artline 70 pen. Also draw in the glass cutting border edge in black.

4. With an Artline 70 pen, red or blue, draw in the border lead lines, directly over the pencil lines. (This will remove approximately 1 mm all around the border to allow for ease of insertion of the panel into its frame—check that you have this space.)
5. Using the same coloured pen, mark in any necessary support lines. Also mark in the directional lines if streaky or one-way pattern glass is being used—Fig. 2.

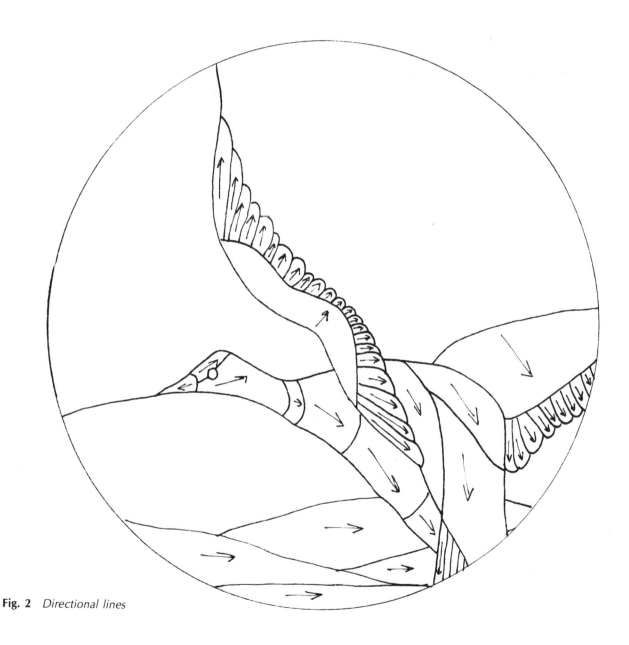

Fig. 2 *Directional lines*

Measuring for a leaded panel

1. Leaded panels fit firmly into the frame.
2. Accurate measurements are important. Check for squareness of the panel, and that oval and circular panels are correct. Make cardboard or thin plywood templates if in doubt. There are few things more upsetting when working in stained glass than to make a truly square panel, or perfect circle or oval, only to find the frame is not perfect in shape. Always check for accuracy by using the glass viewing line. Any imperfections in the frame can be visually corrected by using this line as the correct shape for the panel. The minimum rebate area can be drawn onto this line. The completed panel will not be a perfect fit within the frame, but the lead border on the glass viewing area will be accurate, and will look visually correct. Any area between the leaded panel and the rebate can be packed, if necessary.

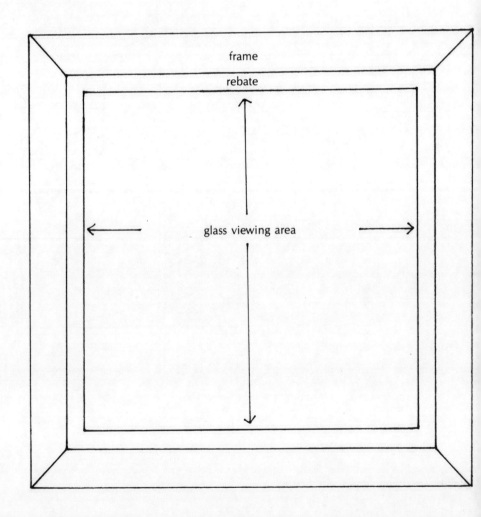

frame

rebate

glass viewing area

Fig. 3 *Total panel size: Rebate + glass viewing area + rebate*

3. Three measurements are needed:
   (a) Total area: the maximum size which will fit firmly into the frame.
   (b) Rebate: the narrow support ridge of the frame that the glass sits in.
   (c) Glass viewing area: the area that is glass only. It is the difference between the total area and the rebate. (See Fig. 3).
4. The rebate measurement determines the size of the border lead. At least 2–3 mm (⅛'') of lead should be visible within the glass viewing area:

       rebate 10 mm = lead 12 mm minimum
       rebate   8 mm = lead 10 mm minimum

   The lead width, not the rebate width, is required for correct construction.

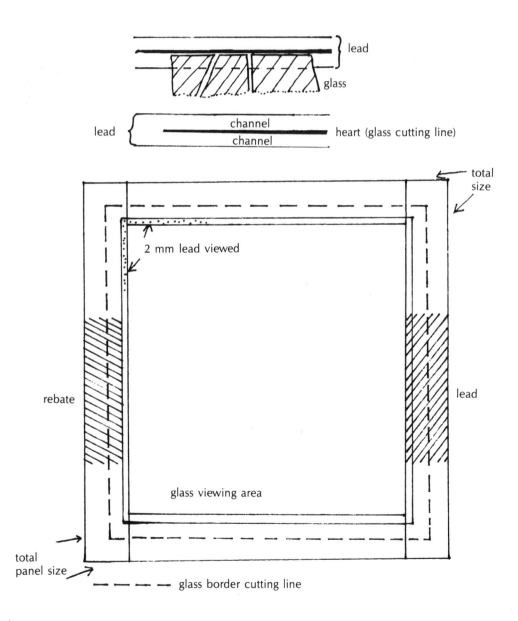

Fig. 4 *Measuring for a leaded panel*

5. It is possible to draw the total panel size in two ways. Use pencil only until all drawing and designing is completed.

Method 1:
(a) Draw up total panel area.
(b) Within this line, draw in lead width.
(c) Divide lead width in halves and draw this line in—this is the glass border cutting line.

Method 2
(a) Measure and draw glass viewing area.
(b) Add rebate measurement all the way round—this gives you total panel size.
(c) Draw up total panel size. Do not draw in rebate line.
(d) Measure and draw in border lead width. Divide lead width in halves, and draw this line—this is your glass cutting line.

Method 2 is the better method if the frame rebate is not accurate.

Cutting glass

1. Place the smooth side of the glass uppermost. Glass is always cut on its smooth side.
2. Cut the glass *inside* the lead lines, *not* on the lead lines. There must be room for the lead to fit between each piece of glass. Number each piece of glass and the corresponding pattern section as you cut. This prevents double cutting or not cutting the piece at all. The glass pieces can also be quickly found during leading by matching the numbers.
3. When all the glass is cut, and fits satisfactorily within the boundaries of the lead lines, prepare for leading-up the panel.

Leading-up a stained glass panel

Leading-up, whether the panel is circular or oval, square or rectangular, must be done inside a fixed wooden jig. This is made by nailing timber strips over the pattern border line to the work board. The timber strips must be cut straight and be flat-edged. Square and rectangular panels need long lengths of timber. Circles and ovals require small pieces so that they will fit neatly on a curved line.

Straight-edged panel
These instructions apply to both square and rectangular panels.
1. Place a straight-edged piece of timber, which is longer than the panel length, to just cover the Artline 70 border line.
2. Place a second straight-edged piece of timber along one side of the panel. If you are right-handed, place it on the left side. If you are left-handed, place it on the right. This will give you a comfortable working position.
3. Place your straightened and opened border lead along these jigs, ensuring the two leads meet neatly at the corner. Do not mitre the corner.

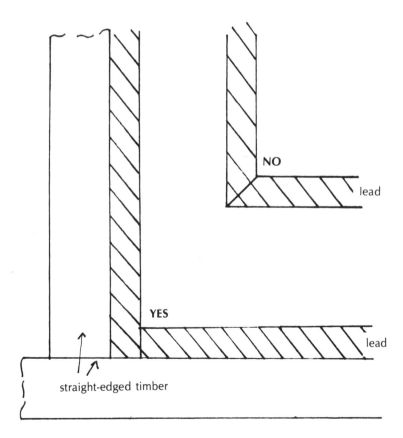

Fig. 5 *Right and wrong way for lead to meet in a corner*

straight-edged timber

4. The first piece of glass is placed in the corner, into the border lead. The inner lead covers the glass edge, and runs from the border lead to the next major intersecting line. Follow the gentlest curving line, and try to use long lines of lead for neat appearance and strength. Continue building the lead and glass, carefully following the pattern line. Hold glass and lead in place with horseshoe nails, removing and replacing as you work.

5. If internal support (restrip) is being used, place it between the lead and the glass, starting at the border edge so that it is hidden by the lead. Overlap slightly where it connects with other restrip. Follow your support lines, bending and cutting the restrip when necessary. If using reinforced lead for support, follow the support lines.

6. Join lead only at other lead joins, for neatness and strength. Cut excess lead back to the previous join if necessary. Small pieces of lead can be used—they need not be wasted.

7. When the panel is completed, and the last two border leads are in place (making certain that the border lead does not cover the outer Artline 70 border lead line), place third and fourth pieces of straight edge to just over the border line. Light tapping of the straight-edge timber with a small hammer may be required to ensure the panel is within the boundary. Using an L-square, check that angles are correct, and firmly nail board into position. Measure width and length to double-check that the panel is 2–3 mm less than the original measurements (allows for ease of insertion into frame).

8. The panel is now ready to be soldered.

Circular and oval panels

1. When working with curved edge panels, depending on the depth of the curved line, only a small part of the outer border lead line will be covered by the straight-edged timber pieces. These should be small enough to give support to the border lead as it follows the curve.

2. Nail the timber pieces in place halfway around the circle. Keep one side open, so that you can work into the open area.

3. Bend the border lead against the timber jig, following the curved border line. Do not cover the outer border lead line, it must be visible.

4. Place glass into the section nearest to you, into the border lead. Cut the inner lead to fit neatly over the edge of the glass. From the border lead follow the lead line to the next major intersecting line. Try to keep lead lines long, for neatness and strength. Continue leading up, working evenly over the panel area towards the open edge of the panel. Hold glass and lead in place with horseshoe nails, removing and replacing as you work.

5. If internal support (restrip) is being used, place it between the lead and the glass, starting from the border edge, so that it is hidden by the glass and lead. Overlap slightly where it connects with other restrip. Follow your support lines, cutting and bending the restrip where necessary. If using reinforced lead for support, follow the support lines.

6. Join lead only at other lead joins, for neatness and strength. Cut excess lead back to the previous join if necessary. Small pieces of lead can be used on other projects—they will not be wasted.

7. When all the glass is in position, gently bend the border lead into position. Hold firmly in place with horseshoe nails, making sure that the outer Artline 70 border line is visible.
Check that diameter is 2–3 mm less than the original measurement (allows for ease of insertion into frame).
The panel is now ready to solder.

Soldering, puttying and cleaning

1. Using a lead knife, lift lead away from glass at joins, and straighten it.
2. Gently brush lead joins with a soft wire brush.
3. Apply flux (oleic acid or stearine wax) to each lead join.
4. Apply solder neatly; do not spread it unnecessarily over the lead. Keep solder to a minimum—the join should be smoothly covered, and the same level as the lead.
5. When the panel is soldered on the first side, carefully turn it over and repeat the procedure given above.
6. Push putty under the lead, and clean away excess with a straight horseshoe nail. Do not miss puttying any sections of lead. Turn panel over.

7. Putty the second side of the panel and clean away excess.
8. Sprinkle a small amount of cleaning compound over the panel and brush over the glass and lead until the excess putty has been removed. Clean up the lead edges with a horseshoe nail. Turn panel over and repeat the procedure. Remove all putty from the lead—do not allow it to dry on the lead.
9. Leave for 24 hours and brush until glass is shining, lead and solder are blackened and all traces of putty are removed.
10. If stay bars (wind bars) are needed, clean off the lead at the predetermined solder points. Cut copper wire in lengths, flux and solder wire to the soldered joints. Clean away the flux and brush the lead to reblacken it.
11. Stove polish can be used to blacken and polish solder and lead. Follow the manufacturer's instructions carefully. Remove all putty from lead before using.

Supporting lead panels

1. Panels larger than 60 cm × 60 cm (2' × 2') must be supported to prevent sagging, bowing and buckling. Panels smaller than the given size may also need support on occasions.
2. The type of support and support lines must be decided on during the drawing stage and be shown on the working cartoon. Support of leaded panels must *never* be an afterthought.
3. Support lines can be straight, or be curved to follow the lead lines, and should be placed approximately every 30 cm (12'').
4. Types of support
   (a) *Restrip:* In leadwork, brass or copper strips are placed between the glass and lead where they are hidden. They follow the lead lines, both vertically and horizontally.
   (b) *Reinforced lead:* Various widths of reinforced lead are available. The metal strengthening rod is inserted within the lead and is also unseen. The reinforced lead is used the same way as ordinary lead.
   (c) *Wind bars:* Also called stay bars. These are thick metal bars 6–10 mm (¼''–½'') in length which are placed into holes in the panel's wooden frame. Wire is soldered to the panel and the metal bars are tied into place with the wire. They are placed in a straight line, horizontally.

4. Blue-faced (or noisy) pitta

5. Blue-winged kookaburras

6. Budgerigars

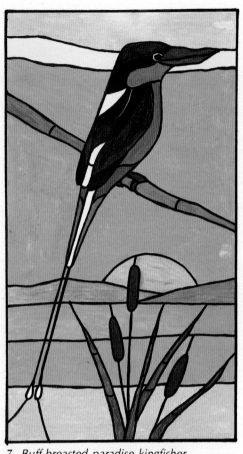

7. Buff-breasted paradise kingfisher

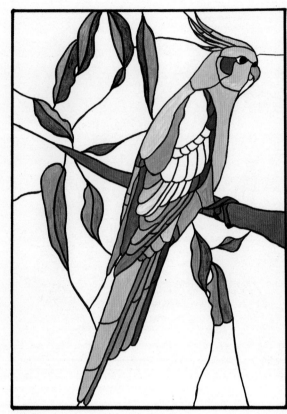

8. Cockatiel

9. Eastern yellow robin (northern variation)

10. Eclectus parrots

11. Galahs

13. King parrots

12. Gouldian finches

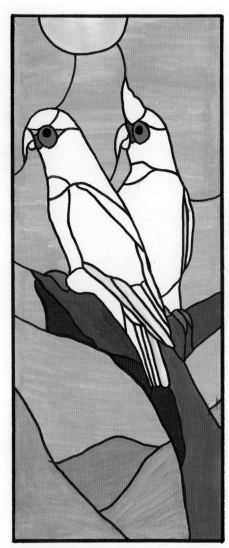

14. *Little-billed corellas*

15. *Orange chats*

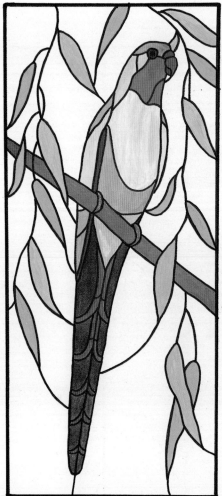

16. *Princess parrot*

Patterns

1. Adelaide rosella

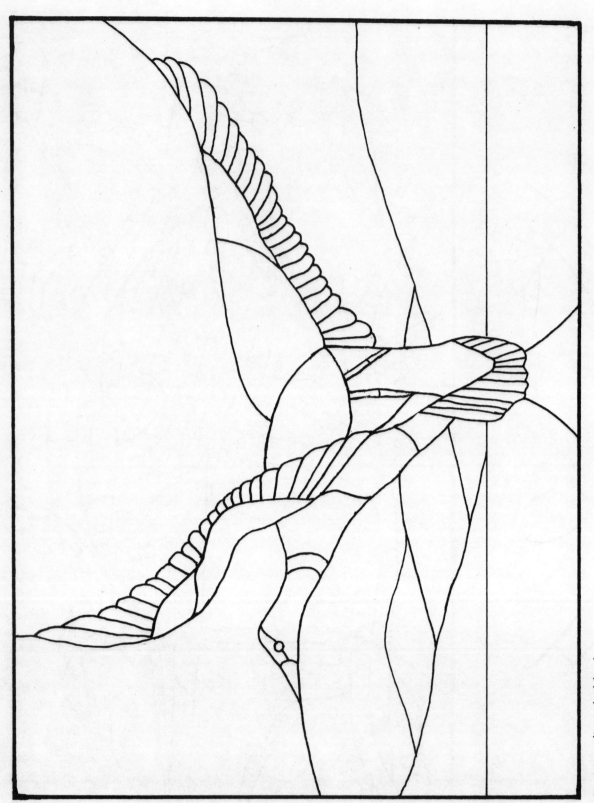

2. Australian shelduck

3. Blue-faced finch

4. Blue-faced (or noisy) pitta

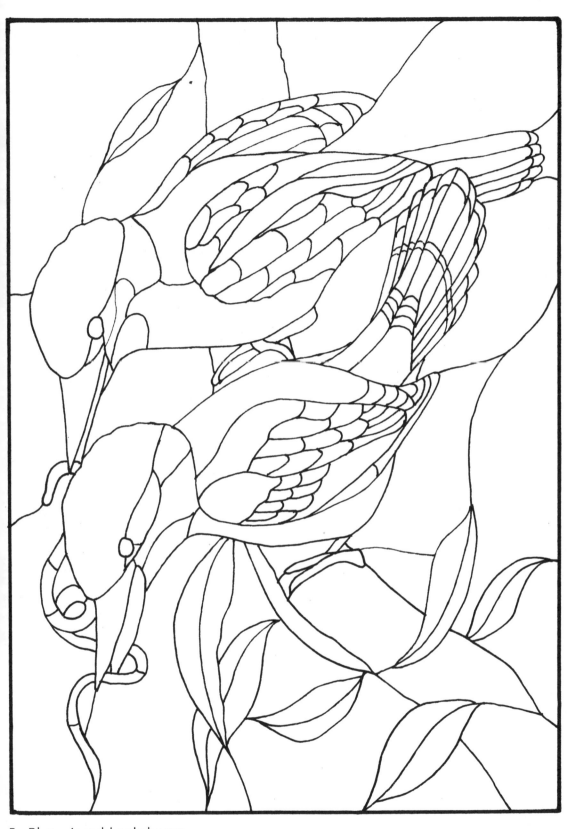

5. Blue-winged kookaburras

6. Budgerigars

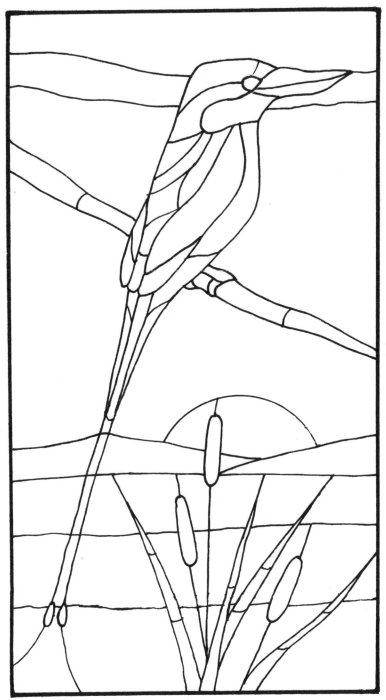

7. Buff-breasted paradise kingfisher

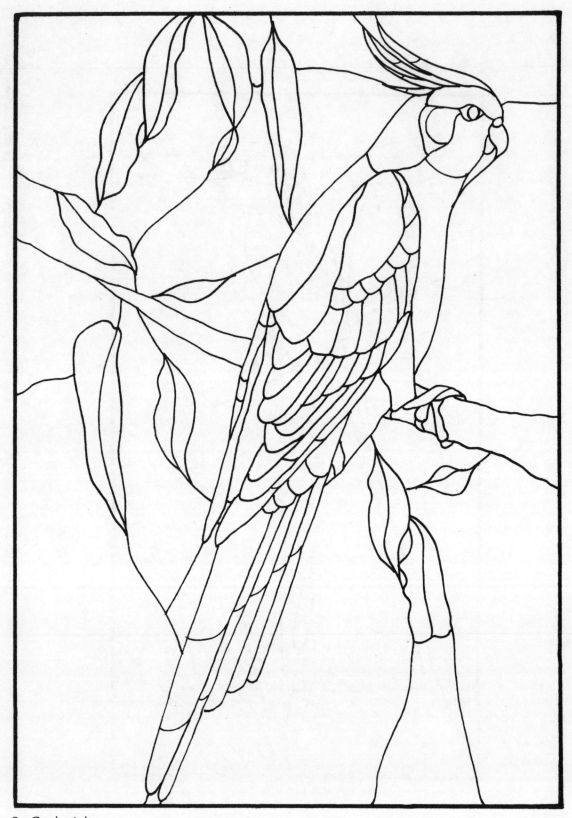

8. Cockatiel

9. Eastern yellow robin (northern variation)

10. Eclectus parrots

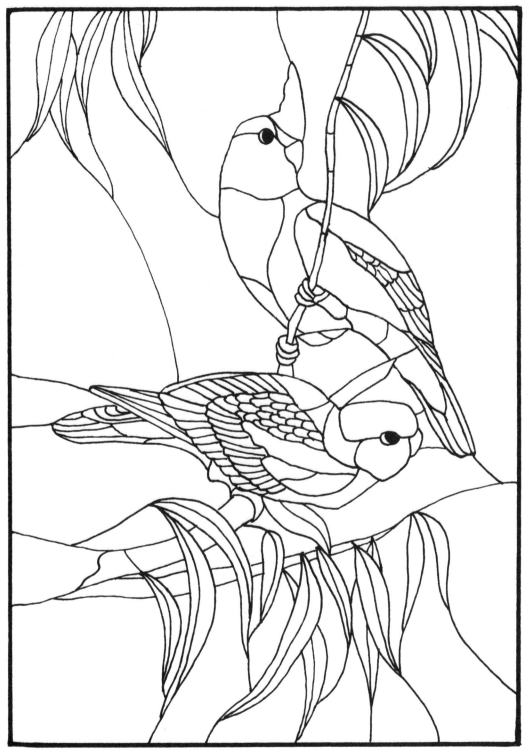

11. Galahs

12. Gouldian finches

13. King parrots

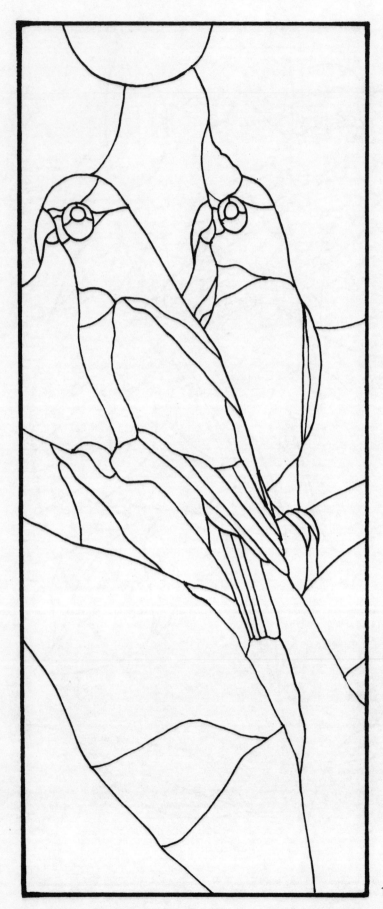

14. Little-billed corellas

15. Orange chats

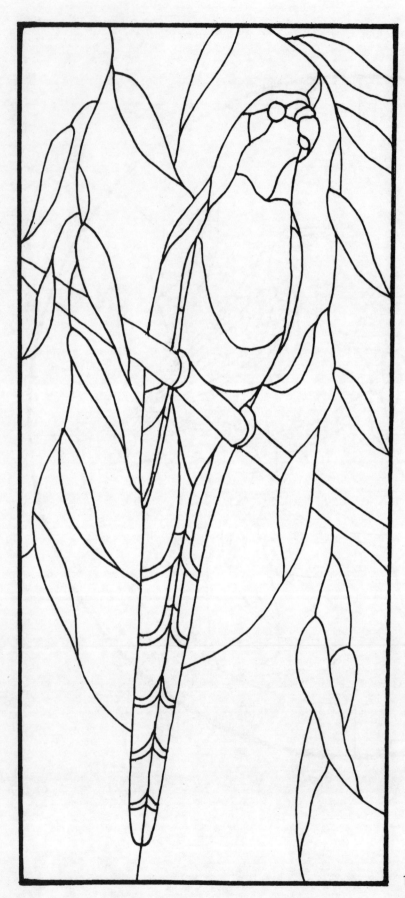

16. Princess parrot

17. Purple-crowned pigeons

18. Purple-crowned wrens

19. Rainbow bee-eater

20. Red-browed firetail

21. Red-collared lorikeet

22. Rufous-crowned emu wrens

23. *Rufous fantails*

24. *Spectacled monarchs*

25. *Sulphur-crested cockatoo*

26. Turquoise parrot

27. Variegated fairy wrens

28. Wedge-tailed eagle

17. Purple-crowned pigeons

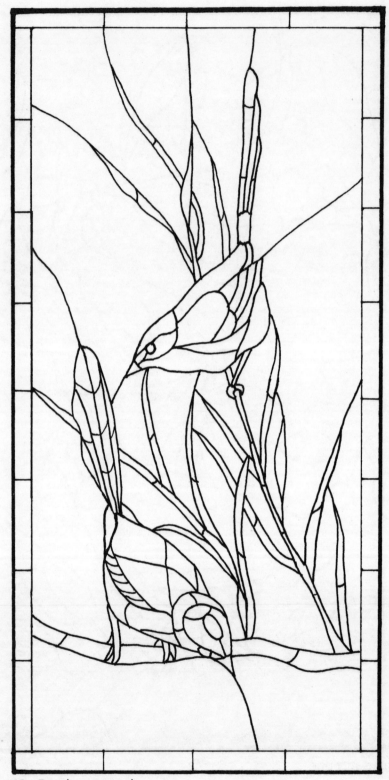

18. Purple-crowned wrens

9. Rainbow bee-eater

20. Red-browed firetail

21. Red-collared lorikeet

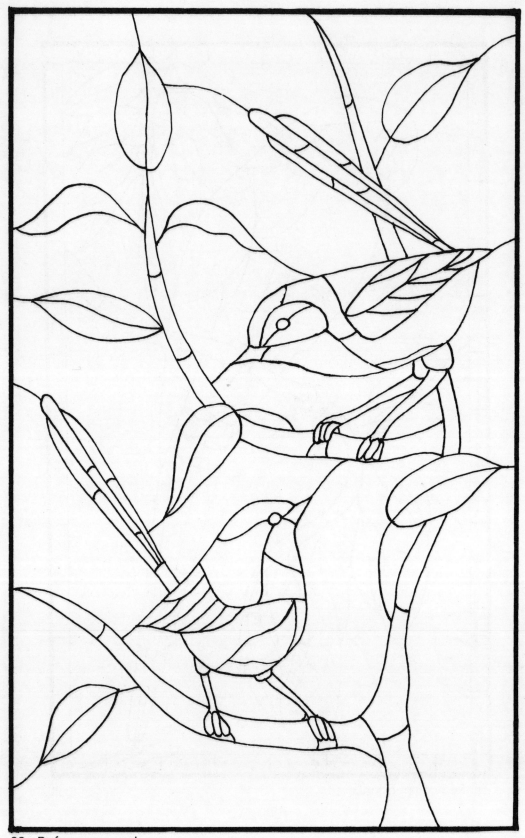

22. Rufous-crowned emu wrens

23. Rufous fantails

24. Spectacled
monarchs

26. Turquoise parrot

27. Variegated fairy wrens

28. Wedge-tailed eagle

29. Western rosella

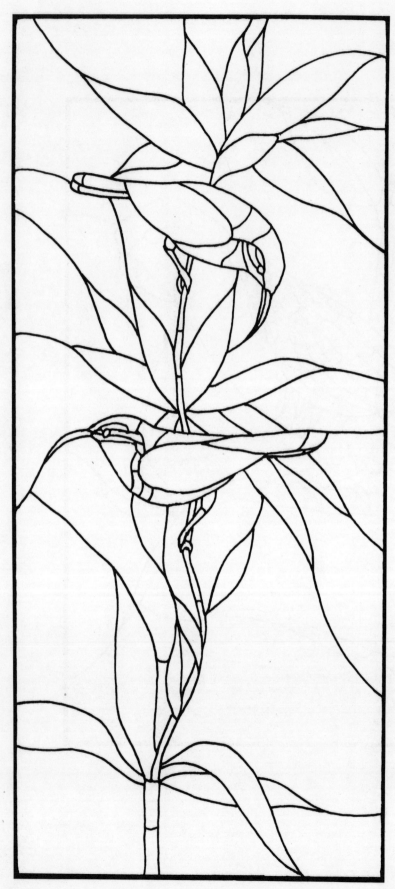

30. Western spinebills

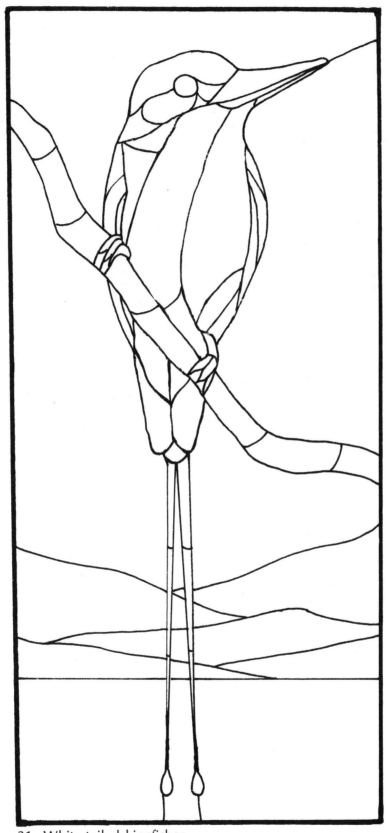

31. White-tailed kingfisher

32. Wompoo fruit-dove